BARGUMENTS

DOUG HANKS

SSE
SIMON SPOTLIGHT ENTERTAINMENT
NEW YORK LONDON TORONTO SYDNEY

SIMON SPOTLIGHT ENTERTAINMENT
An imprint of Simon & Schuster
1230 Avenue of the Americas, New York, New York 10020

Designed by Yaffa Jaskoll
Manufactured in the United States of America
First Edition 10 9 8 7 6 5 4 3
Library of Congress Cataloging-in-Publication Data
Hanks, Doug.
Barguments / Doug Hanks.—1st ed.
p. cm.
ISBN-13: 978-1-4169-5449-1
ISBN-10: 1-4169-5449-X
1. Drinking of alcoholic beverages—Humor. 2. Questions
and answers—Humor. I. Title.
PN6231.D7H36 2007
818'.602—dc 22
2007030809

INTRODUCTION

Winter seemed particularly long and cold one year in Oxford, Maryland, a town so small, it gets by without a traffic light. I was idling through a Saturday night at Latitude 38, a bar by the firehouse, when conversation turned to one of the fancier draft beers served there.

The bartender poured it by pulling on a tap handle molded to look like a bear wrestling a lion. This was one epic, self-important brew. At one point someone asked a simple, life-changing question: Who do you think would win that fight?

Heads looked up. Glasses went down.

"The bear is going to kill the lion," said Eric, a drinking buddy. "He's three times stronger than the lion. He's got reach. The lion won't be able to get near him."

I disagreed. "First of all, the lion's the king of the jungle. Second of all, he'll pounce on the bear and that's the end of the bear."

The debate lasted most of the night, with even the busboy taking sides. Everyone had a theory. And a rebuttal. And a special on the Discovery Channel they'd seen that proved their point.

When summer arrived, someone posed another showstopper: Would you rather give up ice or air-conditioning? I picked ice, even as I reached for another beer from the cooler. Not a popular move among the ice fans.

More questions followed, sparking some pretty fierce barroom arguments. So we started calling them "barguments."

Barguments follow three absolute rules:

1. You can't be proven right or wrong in a bargument, even though it's so clear that you're right and the guy across the bar must be a complete idiot.

2. Barguments involve the important issues of our time: television, junk food, sex, *Star Wars*—you cannot have a bargument about capital punishment or war—unless it's a pretend war between wolves and monkeys.
3. No bargument can be so complicated that you can't get your head around it after three beers.

A bargument shreds small talk and quickly divides people into opposing camps. Think you know someone? Test that premise with a bargument.

SCENARIO NO. 1: I hope you like dogs. I have three Yorkies.

SCENARIO NO. 2: So you're telling me you would give up *dogs* before you would give up *beer*?! That's so cold.

Barguments also can be helpful in professional situations. Mediocre interviewers ask questions like this: Tell me your biggest flaw.

But barguments bring more insight to employment screenings. Would *you* hire someone who thought Superman could beat Aquaman in an underwater race around the world?

Throughout this book you'll find a few extras accompanying the barguments. The "With a Twist" feature nudges a bargument to the next level or asks you to consider a slightly different scenario. "Cocktail Chatter" offers points to consider while barguing, or establishes parameters for the answer.

Occasionally, Eric, my drinking buddy and *Barguments* collaborator, will also pop in with a comment or seek clarification on a bargument. Are we considering mayonnaise a condiment? Does *Pimp My Ride* qualify as a fix-it-up show?

I've included rulings for those, but you'll inevitably have to hammer out other technical issues yourself. The uninitiated tend to panic when asked to make the instant choices barguments demand.

Reassure them with decisiveness. Lay down

your own bargument law—yes, weather forecasters *do* count as television journalists and you may consider them when deciding which TV reporter you want to sleep with—and then let the barguing continue.

Use this book to get to know your social circle a little better. And use it to meet other bar-goers who share your strident views. Remember: Good friends make for the best barguments. Even if it turns out that many of those good friends have no goddamn idea what they're talking about.

Enjoy.

1

Who would win in a fight: a lion or a bear?

BARGU-MOMENT: The original bargument, this quickly divides a crowd into bear and lion camps. One night at Pope's Tavern, an old man at the end of the bar listened to us go back and forth on this one. Then he cleared his throat and declared: "It depends on the environment. If they're in the woods, the bear's going to win. If they're in the jungle? The lion is going to kick the bear's ass."

2

Which sport produces more attractive athletes: swimming or tennis?

If one store could open twenty-five steps from your front door, would you choose a Starbucks, a McDonald's, or a 7-Eleven?

4

Would you rather be allergic to couches or remote controls?

5

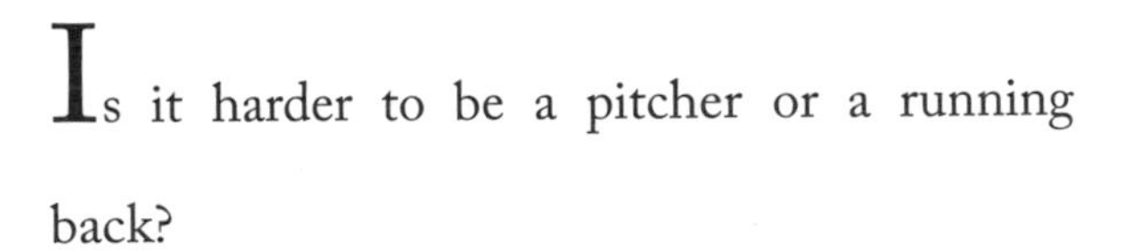

Is it harder to be a pitcher or a running back?

6

Would you rather give up ice cream or pizza?

COCKTAIL CHATTER: And ice cream includes frozen yogurt, sorbet, gelato, and any other frozen dessert you can think of.

7

If you could be free from one task for life, would it be shaving or laundry?

8

Who on *Friends* would be the best in bed?

One thousand dollars ride on a game of H.O.R.S.E. Would you rather bet on Dwayne Wade wearing mittens or on a starter from the varsity team at your high school?

10

You'll be given an all-expenses-paid trip for two with luxury accommodations to the destination of your choice every four years. The catch: You can't take any vacations between the lavish junkets. Do you accept?

If you had to sleep with every member of a band, which group would get lucky?

12

You've bet five thousand dollars on a game of rock, paper, scissors. What do you throw?

13

What is the creepiest pet a person can have?

14

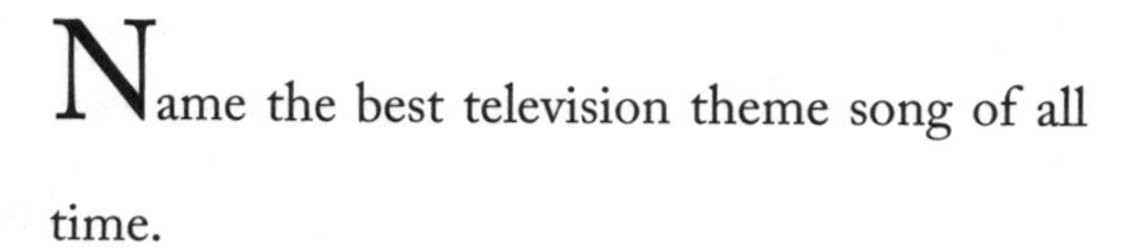

Name the best television theme song of all time.

15

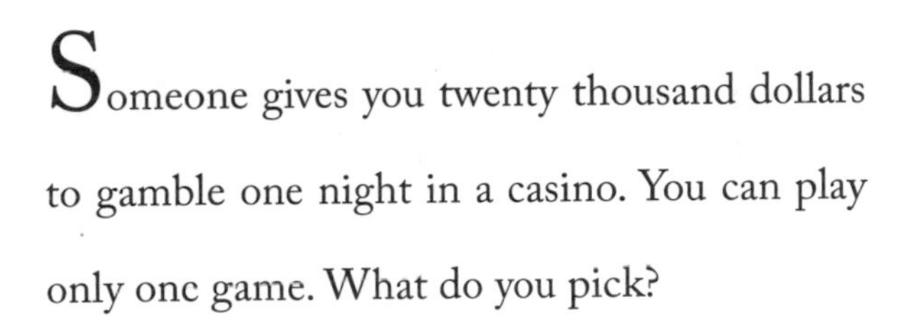

Someone gives you twenty thousand dollars to gamble one night in a casino. You can play only onc game. What do you pick?

Which commercial would you ban from ever airing again?

17

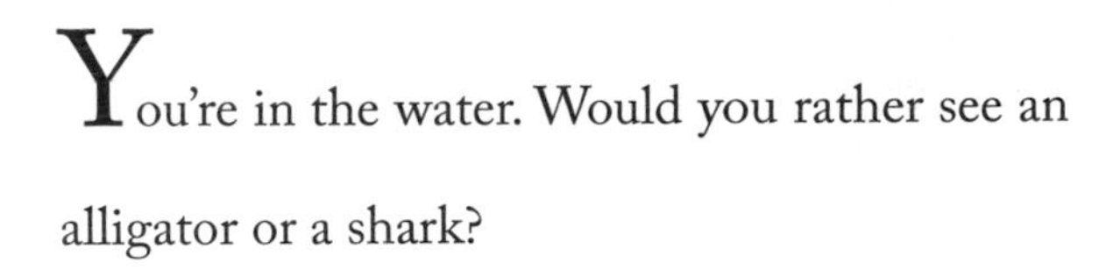

You're in the water. Would you rather see an alligator or a shark?

18

Would you rather give up television or alcohol?

ERIC: Could you still watch DVDs on your television?
DOUG: Yes, but not DVDs of TV shows.

19

You'll be restricted to patronizing one bar for the next twelve months. What's your pick?

20

If you could be cast in any reality show, which would you pick?

21

What's the most exciting sports event of the year?

22

If the snooze button on your alarm clock charged one dollar per use, would you push it?

23

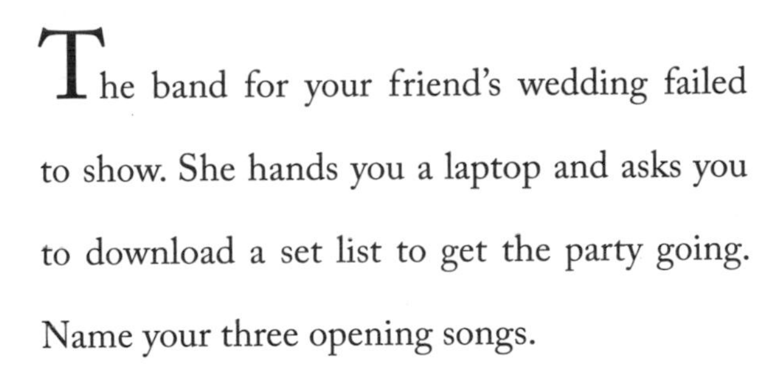

The band for your friend's wedding failed to show. She hands you a laptop and asks you to download a set list to get the party going. Name your three opening songs.

24

Would you drop ten pounds in exchange for instantly aging a year?

25

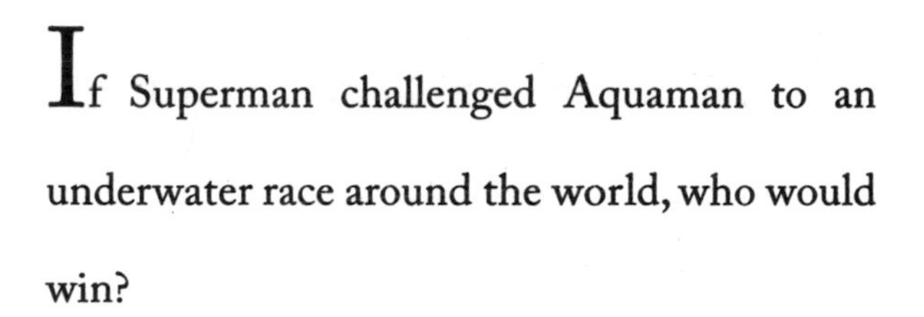

If Superman challenged Aquaman to an underwater race around the world, who would win?

26

Which fast-food chain makes the best burgers?

27

How much would you pay to see your favorite dead musician play one more concert?

28

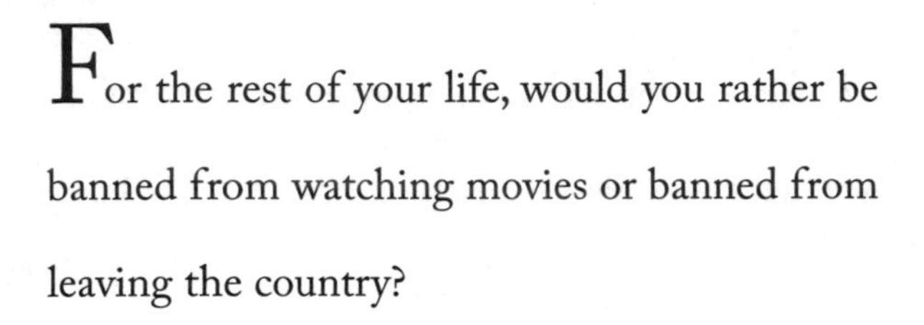

For the rest of your life, would you rather be banned from watching movies or banned from leaving the country?

29

Which season would you eliminate?

30

With a million dollars at stake, would you rather shoot a free throw or flip a coin?

31

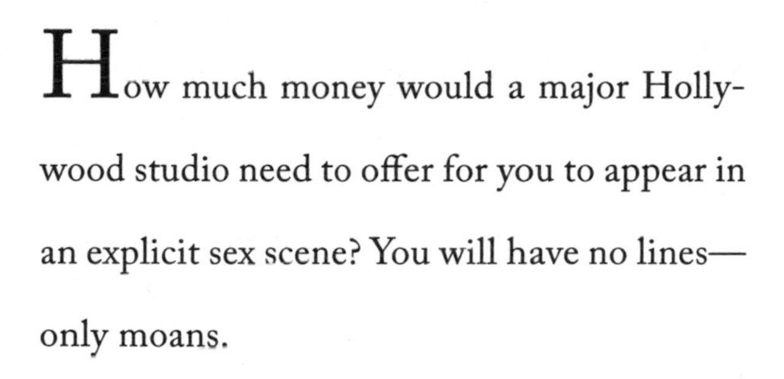

How much money would a major Hollywood studio need to offer for you to appear in an explicit sex scene? You will have no lines—only moans.

32

Who has the best pizza in town?

Choose one of these rules to obey for the next fourteen days: going for a hug every time someone offers you a handshake, or ending all telephone conversations with "Love ya."

34

Who would win in a war: Texas or California?

COCKTAIL CHATTER: Sure, Texans love their guns. But so do the Crips.

Someone has left a twenty-dollar bill floating in the toilet in a public restroom. The water appears clean. What do you do?

With a Twist: Would your answer change if it was a five or a fifty?

What's the greatest sports movie of all time?

You've been kidnapped. You can call on the characters from one television show to make a rescue attempt. Which show do you pick?

38

Would you rather gain fifty pounds and be allowed to drive cars, or maintain your current weight but be barred from getting behind the wheel?

39

Which would you rather give up for six months: sex or alcohol?

40

You've been sentenced to thirty years in prison and can subscribe to one magazine. What's your pick?

Would you rather give up elevators or electric car windows?

42

Which celebrity has aged the best?

43

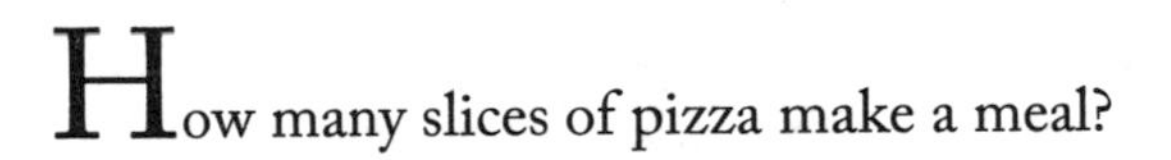

How many slices of pizza make a meal?

Rank these sitcoms from best to worst: *Frasier*, *That '70s Show*, *Family Guy*, *The Office*, *Reno 911!*

Rank the seven continents in order of the best places to vacation.

46

You're stuck in an elevator for two hours. Would you rather be alone or with a stranger?

With a Twist: What if you had a newspaper with you?

47

Name the five best bands of all time.

Would you rather have a private bathroom at work or a hot tub at home?

With a Twist: What if you had to choose between a hot tub at home and a private bathroom wherever you went?

49

Who enjoys sex more: men or women?

50

You have a new brother-in-law and get to select his occupation. Pick from rock star, doctor, and carpenter.

51

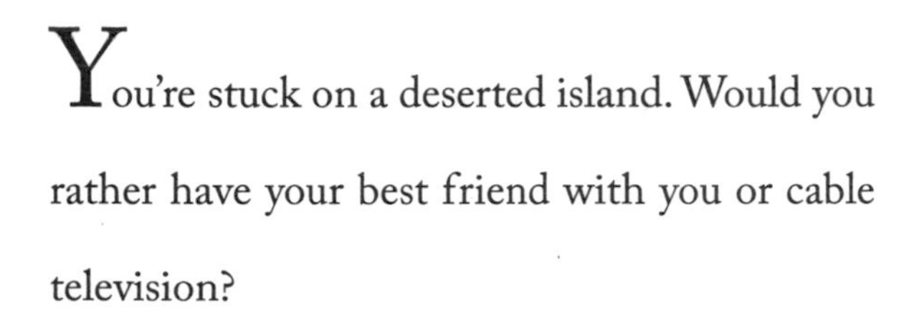

You're stuck on a deserted island. Would you rather have your best friend with you or cable television?

COCKTAIL CHATTER: Don't try to claim that you're dating or married to your best friend. It's got to be your official, nonsexual best friend.

52

Which bar serves the best buffalo wings?

53

How many times can you wear jeans without washing them?

54

What's the most overrated movie?

55

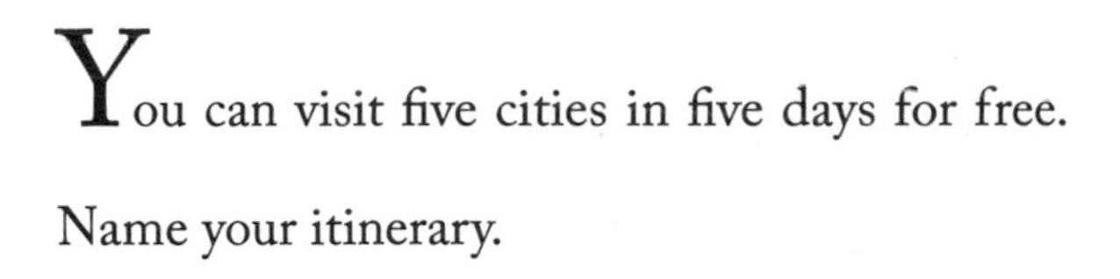

You can visit five cities in five days for free.

Name your itinerary.

COCKTAIL CHATTER: You fly by private jet, but actual travel times still apply.

56

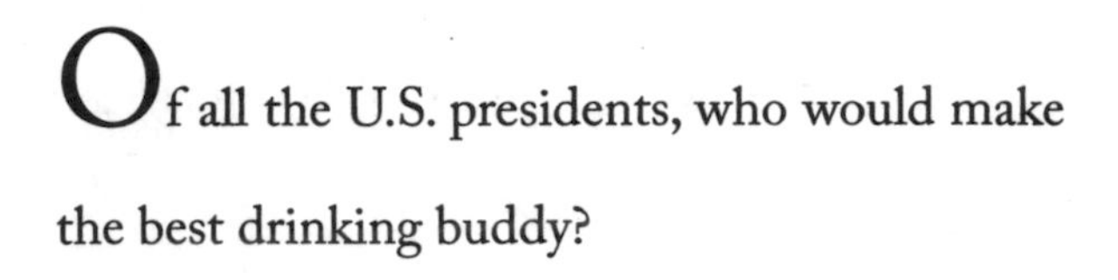

Of all the U.S. presidents, who would make the best drinking buddy?

ERIC: I'm going with Andrew Jackson.
DOUG: What would make you say Andrew Jackson?
ERIC: He just seems like a mean old bastard who's not fooling around when it comes to drinking. You know Old Hickory's going to have a still out back.

57

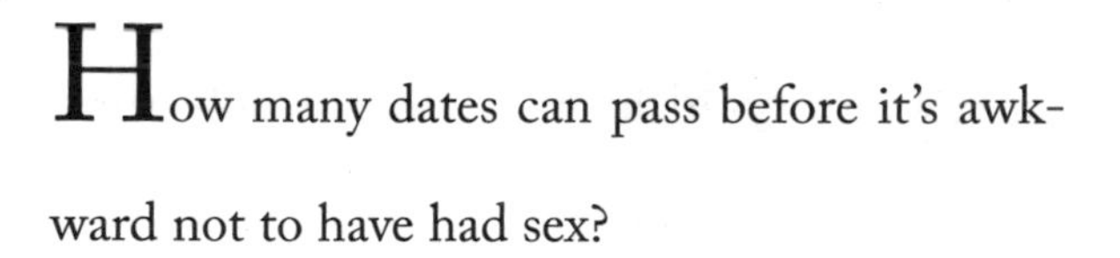

How many dates can pass before it's awkward not to have had sex?

Televisions will be restricted to only three channels. Pick them.

59

You can press a button and do one of three things after sex without any chance of negative consequences. Pick from: go to sleep, instantly be alone in your bed, or have sex again in twenty minutes.

60

If you could date a cartoon character, who would it be?

61

Which profession requires the most knowledge: auto mechanic, chef, or pilot?

62

If you could collect royalties from any single invention, which would you choose?

63

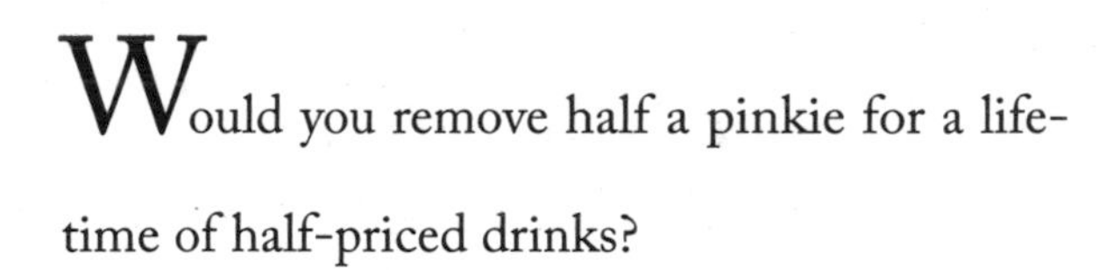

Would you remove half a pinkie for a lifetime of half-priced drinks?

ERIC: I don't see a downside. You get cheap drinks forever, plus you've got this great war story to tell when someone asks you what happened to your finger.

64

Pick the winners in these chess matches:

Bill Clinton versus Hillary Clinton

Cal Ripken Jr. versus Kobe Bryant

Britney Spears versus Ozzy Osbourne

65

Which professional sport is hardest to coach?

Would you rather be a rich idiot or a poor genius?

You'll earn one hundred dollars a point on an SAT exam. Who do you want to take the test: Nicole Richie, Courtney Love, or Keith Richards?

68

Which is funnier: *The Daily Show* or *The Colbert Report*?

Would you rather give up sex with other people or switch sexual orientations?

70

Your life depends on Tiger Woods missing. Do you want him to attempt a three-point shot alone on a basketball court, or a twenty-five-yard putt while you're making out with his wife at the edge of the green?

71

Would you rather give up wine or chocolate?

72

What's the best song from:

The Rolling Stones

Schoolhouse Rock cartoons

The 1980s

A boy band

Television commercials

73

Would you rather give up radio in the car or reading in the bathroom?

74

Name the three most crucial body parts (in order) when it comes to personal appearance.

75

Would you rather face a tsunami or an avalanche?

76

Which country would you pick to be the source of all your beer?

COCKTAIL CHATTER: Keep in mind that you'd still need to go through normal retail outlets to purchase it.

You must deliver a long, hearty lick to one of these surfaces. Choose from a subway pole, the water dish in a dog kennel, or the top of your bathroom trash can.

78

Would you rather fast for three days or run a marathon?

ERIC: Do you have to actually finish the marathon?
DOUG: You'd have to either finish or run until you collapse.

Which U.S. city has the best food?

With a Twist: Which has the best music?

In your dream kitchen would you rather have a beer tap or a Slurpee machine?

From now on at professional sporting events you can eat only one thing. What would it be?

COCKTAIL CHATTER: And it has to be sold at the stadium. No picking broiled lobster-tail poppers.

82

Would you rather scrub Rush Limbaugh's toilet for a week or scrub his feet?

With a Twist: What if it was Rosie O'Donnell?

83

If they both paid the same, would you rather be a proctologist or a garbage hauler?

84

You can have any product advertised on an infomercial delivered to your home tomorrow at no charge. Which one do you want?

If you had to tap a president from film or television to run the country, who would get the nod?

COCKTAIL CHATTER: Consider these candidates: *West Wing*'s Jed Bartlet, Harrison Ford in *Air Force One*, *24*'s David Palmer, and Chris Rock in *Head of State*.

86

Would you rather put half a cup of sand in your bed or a half teaspoon of gravel in your shoes?

Name the weakest of these shows: *CHiPs*, *MacGyver*, *The A-Team*, or *The Dukes of Hazzard*.

88

List the top three guitar players in history.

89

Would you rather get a 20-percent raisc or work a four-day week?

If you wanted to risk being the most-egged house on the block, what candy should you hand out for Halloween?

91

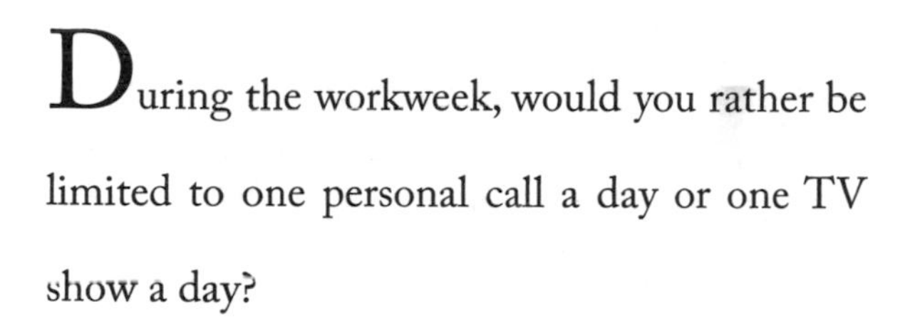

During the workweek, would you rather be limited to one personal call a day or one TV show a day?

92

You're trapped in a mine shaft, and the industrial elevator won't work. You can have one team with you. Do you want the guys from *MythBusters* or the guys from *American Chopper*?

93

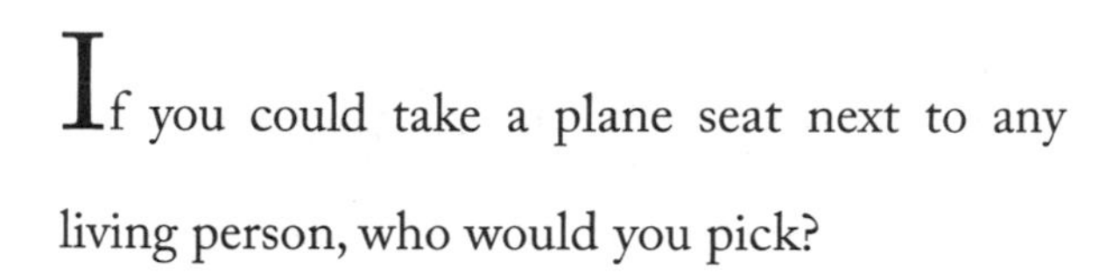

If you could take a plane seat next to any living person, who would you pick?

COCKTAIL CHATTER: Be sure to consider who would actually talk to you during a flight.

Would you rather be deathly allergic to dogs or to beer?

95

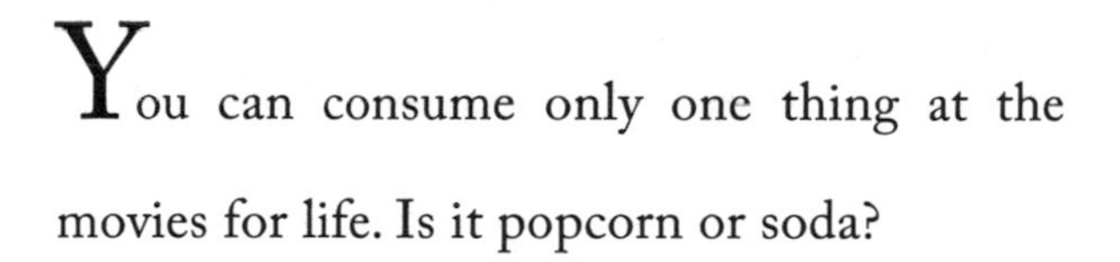

You can consume only one thing at the movies for life. Is it popcorn or soda?

If you could score free tickets and transportation to any awards show, which one would you attend?

97

Would you rather give up coffee or soda?

98

In the Batman movies who is the coolest villain?

99

Rank these bands from best to worst: Aerosmith, Bon Jovi, Def Leppard, Guns N' Roses, Van Halen.

100

You have a pistol with one bullet. Would you rather face an angry wolf or an angry cobra?

101

What song do you play on the jukebox if you absolutely want the entire bar to sing along?

102

Name the best fast-food chain in the country.

You can have sex with one television journalist. Who do you pick?

104

Who is the better songwriter: Bob Marley or Jimmy Buffett?

105

What's the least fun month of the year?

106

If you could have sex with any character from an HBO series, who would it be?

Rank the past five decades by their music.

108

Is basketball, baseball, or football more entertaining to watch on television?

With a Twist: What about to watch in person?

Would you rather give up text messages or television news?

110

From now on your car stereo will play only one genre of music. Pick between rap and country.

Which professional baseball team has the most die-hard fans?

112

Would you rather give up drive-through windows or food delivery?

113

Which makes for more fun at a wedding reception: bands or DJs?

114

You can add inches to your chest and take away inches from your waist. But you'll have to shrink your height by one inch for every change you make. What do you do?

Which movie did the best job at being scary *and* believable?

Which song would you ban from wedding receptions?

117

Which is more fun: high school or college?

Would you rather give up music or alcohol?

119

Which game requires more hand-eye coordination: foosball, Skee-Ball, or Madden NFL video game football?

Would you rather run naked through an office holiday party or through your family's next holiday dinner?

121

You have five thousand dollars to spend in one store. Where do you go?

At what age are women usually the most attractive? Men?

Which superhero made the lamest leap from comic books to the movies?

124

Would you rather be an expert in karate, piano, or auto repair?

125

What was the best *Seinfeld* episode?

126

If you couldn't use firearms or explosives, what weapon would you pick for a fight to the death?

127

Would you rather date someone twenty pounds overweight or twenty pounds underweight?

128

You're about to move into an apartment with extremely thin walls. Pick your neighbor: a bass player, a sex addict, or a parrot breeder.

You can have an expense-free trip to the beach destination of your choice. The catch: If you're female, you must go topless; if male, you have to wear a G-string bathing suit. Do you go?

With a Twist: What if your parents went on the trip with you?

130

Would you rather have Fridays or Mondays off from work?

131

If you had to move to another country for life and never leave, where would you go?

132

Would you rather go to bed with three rats in your room or three snakes?

With a Twist: What if you knew none are rabid or poisonous?

133

You'll have only one source of reading material for the rest of your life. Do you want paperback romance novels, comic books, or foreign policy journals?

134

Pick one television chef to cook dinner for you every night.

Would you rather give up air-conditioning or ice?

136

How long is too long to be dating someone without a proposal?

137

Who make better bosses: men or women?

138

Which is the best of the television Christmas specials?

139

Would you rather give up beer or televised sports?

ERIC: Could I keep beer and go to live sporting events?
DOUG: Definitely.
ERIC: Done.

140

Which is worse: ear hair or nose hair?

141

Which *Simpsons* character most deserves a spin-off?

142

After drinking radioactive beer, you've developed a superpower. Pick from extraordinary hearing that lets you listen in whenever someone mentions your name or the ability to instantly detect lies told by strangers.

143

Who talks about sex more: men or women?

144

Which coach, teacher, or principal from the movies most deserved a punch in the face?

145

What was the best movie with:

Morgan Freeman?

Harrison Ford?

Tom Cruise?

Jamie Foxx?

146

What is the blandest ethnic food?

What's the maximum amount of credit cards your table can turn in with the check without seeming completely obnoxious to the waitress?

148

You're trapped in a box. Would you rather have someone put one harmless tarantula inside or twenty black ants?

Four rappers—Snoop Dogg, Eminem, Jay-Z, and Kanye West—will compete in an Ultimate Fighting Championship. Who will be the last man standing?

150

Which is worse on a man: baldness or back hair?

Would you rather be banned from listening to musicians older than you or younger than you?

If you could vacation in only one U.S. state, which would it be?

153

Who deserves the title of Funniest Stand-up Comedian of All Time?

What's the lamest event aired on ESPN?

COCKTAIL CHATTER: Keep in mind that the network broadcasts Scrabble tournaments.

Would you rather be able to see through walls or hear through walls?

156

Who are better athletes: gymnasts or soccer players?

157

A wild boar charges you. Pick a weapon: sword or crossbow.

158

Would you rather give up air travel or meat?

Which perk would you like from a super-VIP card: the privilege of getting your first drink "comped" at any bar; the right to cut in front of the line in any store; or the clout to be whisked past the velvet ropes of any club?

160

Which is harder to hit well: a golf ball or a tennis ball?

161

Would you rather give up caffeine or dessert?

162

What's the smartest breed of dog?

163

Which is more entertaining to watch:

Summer Olympics or Winter Olympics?

World Series or Super Bowl?

College basketball or pro basketball?

Men's tennis or women's tennis?

A boxing match or a hockey brawl?

164

Should Christmas trees have colored lights or white lights?

165

Who would win in an arm-wrestling match: Andy Roddick or Tiger Woods?

166

If the government let you legalize one drug, which—if any—would you pick?

You can't ever drink again in one of these situations. Pick from weddings, vacations, or sporting events.

168

If you had to live in a house from television, which would you pick?

What was the best team to ever win the Super Bowl?

170

You can be free of one thing for life: gas, hangovers, or sleep. Which do you pick?

ERIC: Gas like fuel or gas like gas?
DOUG: Gas like gas.

171

Who would win in a fight between the X-Men and the Fantastic Four?

172

If you could marry into any family, which would you choose?

173

Which is more of a sport: sailing or NASCAR?

174

Who qualifies as television's sexiest medical professional?

You've been sentenced to one year of solitary confinement. Which five CDs would you bring with you?

176

Rank these five comedies from best to worst: *There's Something About Mary*, *Borat*, *Old School*, *Spinal Tap*, *Austin Powers: International Man of Mystery*.

If you were forced to audition for *American Idol*, what song would you sing?

178

As part of a promotion, you're offered a ticket to the Super Bowl, including airfare and lodging. The catch: You must paint your body in team colors and sit in your underwear on the fifty-yard line. Do you go?

You can have any animal from television or film as your pet. Who do you pick?

180

What first name sounds the toughest?

181

If a professional basketball team played a professional soccer team in football, who would win?

With a Twist: What if a baseball team played a hockey team in basketball?

182

You've been sentenced to appear in a reality show on the following list, but the judge will let you strike one from consideration. Do you eliminate *Survivor*, *The Bachelor*, or *Dancing with the Stars*?

Name the coolest superhero of all time.

184

A trainer is willing to take care of an animal for you. So pick a new exotic pet: a monkey, a tiger, or a dolphin.

Which produces sharper political commentary: *The Simpsons* or *South Park*?

For one year would you rather give up talking on cell phones or watching television shows?

You can instantly be a master at any musical instrument. Which do you pick?

188

Would you rather drink a glass of melted butter or eat a small bowl of mayonnaise?

Which is more fun: Friday night or Saturday night?

190

From now on you must stay home and read for one of these holidays. Pick between New Year's Eve and Fourth of July.

You're vacationing in a remote, all-inclusive resort. Who do you want to be booked unexpectedly in the room next door: an ex or your boss?

192

Would you rather date someone with a thick accent from New York or from Arkansas?

Who would win this race: Tara Reid changing a tire, Gwyneth Paltrow chugging a twelve-pack of beer, or Sheryl Crow finishing a five-hundred-piece jigsaw puzzle?

194

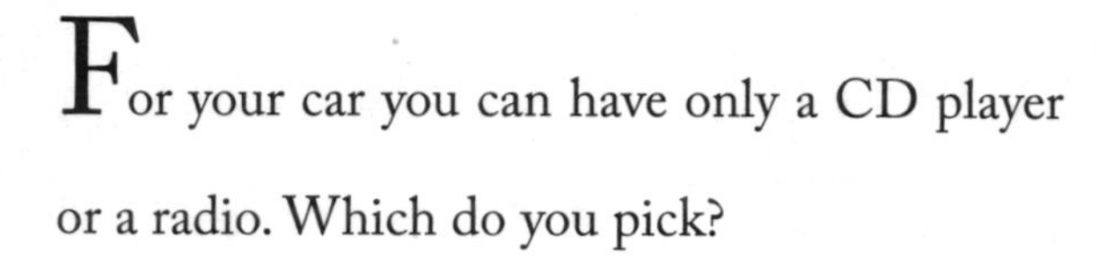

For your car you can have only a CD player or a radio. Which do you pick?

If you were limited to one curse word for life, which would you choose?

ERIC: Damn.
DOUG: Is that your answer?
ERIC: No, I was saying, "Damn, that's a tough one."

196

You're marooned on an uncharted island. The characters from one sitcom will share your fate. Pick them.

197

Would you rather be forced to give up e-mail or salt?

198

You suddenly have the ability to implant a song in your enemies' heads. Which one do you pick?

Which is more of a sport: cheerleading or bowling?

200

True or false: The more attractive the person, the less aggressive they are in bed.

Which was the superior movie franchise: *The Lord of the Rings*, *Star Wars*, or *The Matrix*?

202

Starting tomorrow, you must trade places with a celebrity. Whose famous life would you like?

Which R-rated movie has the best sex scene?

You can have only one condiment for the rest of your life. Which do you pick?

ERIC: Are you considering mayonnaise a condiment?
DOUG: Yes. Same with ketchup.
ERIC: What about salad dressing?
DOUG: That's a separate category.
ERIC: Hot sauce?
DOUG: Condiment.

Which is more impressive: a no-hitter or a hole in one?

206

Which show had better acting: *Baywatch* or *Saved by the Bell*?

207

If you had to give up the fork, the knife, or the spoon, which utensil would you surrender?

208

If the Olympics added a new sport, which one would get the best ratings: dodgeball, extreme skateboarding, or Texas Hold'em poker?

Where's the sexiest spot on a woman for a tattoo? What about on a man?

COCKTAIL CHATTER: "Nowhere" counts as an answer.

210

Pick an animal to be attacked by: a crazed dog or a crazed monkey.

211

Would you rather be a school bus driver or a city bus driver?

You have to stick your head in a bucket for thirty seconds. Do you fill it with fish guts, horse urine, or roaches?

213

What's the best-ever:

Drinking game?

Guitar riff?

Beer commercial?

Trick play?

Car chase scene?

Would you rather take public transportation to work every day or be required to walk everywhere on your days off?

If you had to go into a steel cage match with one of these men in their prime, would it be an angry Mike Tyson, an angry Muhammad Ali, or an angry Bruce Lee?

Pick a spot for a new twenty-four-hour web-cam: in your bedroom or in your bathroom?

Would you rather give up chocolate or cheese?

218

Who would win in a mob war between Michael Corleone and Tony Soprano?

Would you rather give up shorts or sunglasses?

With a Twist: What about sunglasses or swimming?

You'll be chained to a celebrity for one month. Pick from 50 Cent, Rachael Ray, or Michael Moore.

Would you rather give up listening to music in the car or listening to live music?

What's the all-time best stripping song?

Would you accept $50 million to never have intercourse again?

Which of these shows has the most believable plots: *The X-Files*, *Lost*, or *24*?

225

You'll win one million dollars as long as you don't finish last in the race. Do you want to compete in the Kentucky Derby or the Olympic luge finals?

226

Would you rather be stranded on an island with a motorboat anchored two miles out or marooned in the desert with a car parked fifteen miles away?

227

You have a two-hour wait ahead of you at a doctor's office. Which magazine do you want to be sitting on the table?

228

The world will have access to only three pizza toppings. Pick them.

Would you rather face a charging bull or a swarm of killer bees?

230

One equals painfully bad. Ten equals a TiVo must. Score these shows:

My Name Is Earl

Smallville

Deadliest Catch

COPS

The Soup

231

Pick the best athlete out of this group: Roger Federer, Tom Brady, or Lance Armstrong.

232

You must replace all of your televisions with a new model. Pick from: a TV that receives only broadcast networks but has a remote control or a TV with satellite reception but no remote.

Would you rather give up all cell-phone conversations while driving or be forced to drive the speed limit?

234

Who likes their friends more: men or women?

Name the grossest item on the menu of any major fast-food chain.

236

Would you rather be able to breathe underwater or become invisible?

If you could instantly become five times better at doing one thing, what would you choose?

COCKTAIL CHATTER: You must pick a task, not a result. "Making money" would not be acceptable, for example, but "selling cars" would.

238

What's worse: the limp handshake, the sweaty handshake, or the iron-grip handshake?

From now on you can eat one food without any negative consequences. Which one would you pick?

240

Name the five best sitcoms of all time.

Would you rather be hit in the shoulder with an orange thrown by a college baseball player, a tennis ball served by Venus Williams, or a golf club swung by Ashlee Simpson?

Rank these cartoons: *ThunderCats*, *G.I. Joe*, *He-Man*, *Jonny Quest*, *Speed Racer*.

Would you chop off two fingers to win free Super Bowl tickets for life?

When are you too old to do a beer bong?

With a Twist: What about playing Quarters?

Would you rather give up earphones or bottled water?

246

Who was the better singer: Kurt Cobain or Jerry Garcia?

You've been accused of murder. You can pick one attorney from television to represent you. Who do you hire?

Which show offers the slimmest chance of winning big: *Deal or No Deal*, *Wheel of Fortune*, or *The Amazing Race*?

250

Would you accept one hundred thousand dollars to never read another book?

With a Twist: What if it was two hundred thousand dollars to give up video games?

Which movie has the best sound track?

251

You have to eat lunch in the same restaurant for the next six months. What do you pick?

COCKTAIL CHATTER: Remember that you'll have to pay the tab each time.

252

Would you rather date someone with three lip rings or feathered hair?

Would you rather be a star musician, a star athlete, or a movie star?

254

Who conducts the more revealing interviews: Ali G or Borat?

One of these guys will join you as a drinking buddy. Do you want Derek Jeter, Conan O'Brien, or Willie Nelson?

Which would you rather give up during the weekends: sex, television, or alcohol?

257

Which is worse: shoveling snow or picking dog poop?

258

Your cell phone must lose one feature. Pick caller ID or voice mail.

Who would make the better flatmate: Prince William or Prince Harry?

260

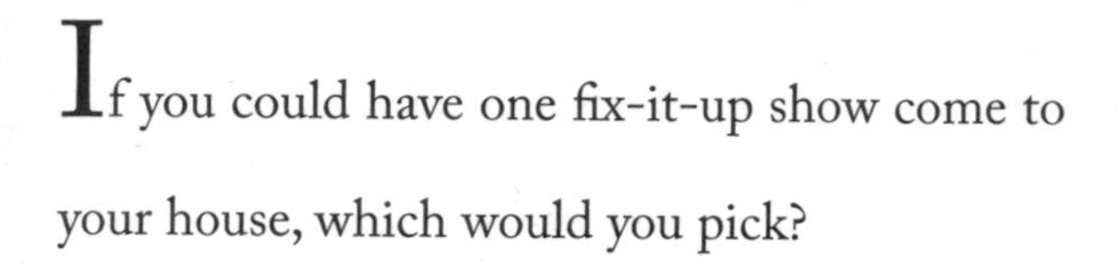

If you could have one fix-it-up show come to your house, which would you pick?

ERIC: Including *Pimp My Ride*?
DOUG: That's a good one. And it qualifies.

261

You've won the lottery. Do you want a check for one million dollars tomorrow, or twelve yearly installments of one hundred thousand dollars?

262

If you had to pierce a part of your body other than an ear, what would it be?

263

Which child star made the most impressive transition into an adult career?

Rank these sports from hardest to easiest: field hockey, lacrosse, soccer.

Which was the best *Saturday Night Live* cast?

266

They've invented an autopilot for your car, but it will allow you to perform only one task while you're not driving. Do you want to make it reading, typing, or watching television?

Would you rather lose your sense of taste for sweet and salty foods or gain weight at triple the normal rate?

268

Which college basketball coach stands out as the best in history?

269

Would you rather be trapped overnight in a blizzard or in a Category Two hurricane?

270

What's the sexiest accent?

271

Would you rather be limited to paying twenty dollars for haircuts, dinner entrées, or bottles of wine?

272

Judging them by their entire movie careers, who is funniest: Eddie Murphy, Mike Myers, or Ben Stiller?

273

Who would win a fight between:

Jason Bourne and James Bond?

Neo and Harry Potter?

Yoda and Spider-Man?

274

What's the best bargument?

ACKNOWLEDGMENTS

If ink didn't smudge so easily on cocktail napkins, this book would have come out sooner.

Many of these barguments came to life more than a decade ago. Sitting at a bar and watching the Weather Channel, I hear someone five stools down wonder if a hurricane would be worse than a blizzard. Forty-five minutes later, the blizzard haters win the vote by a slim margin. Credit bargument No. 269 to that wasted afternoon.

So I have many contributors to thank here, but many, many more to snub. Not intentionally, of course. Memories were a frequent casualty to the *Barguments* creative process. I vaguely recall a classic involving Vanilla Ice and a pack of coyotes. But the nuances escape me, as does the creator. My apologies.

Let me acknowledge those I can.

If you like this book, thank Eric Abell. He and I originally hashed out the idea for *Barguments*. Many of the best ones in here are his, and he brought an eye for grade-A barguments to the project. Eric believes in pared-down fun: Put some friends around a cooler and laughs will follow. Barguments rest on the same premise. If you have half as much fun with them as we all did up in the Gut Hut, this will be a bestseller.

Thanks to my stepfather, John Stalfort, for serving as the unofficial *Barguments* attorney. He gives me the best kind of legal advice: expert and free. Elizabeth, my sister, did a great job prodding me to make deadline. I wouldn't chop off a finger for Super Bowl tickets, but I just might do so to have her work ethic.

Lee Ann Chearney and Gene Brissie get thanks as early believers in *Barguments*. So does Michael Nagin, both for creating a brilliant book cover and for putting my name on a bar coaster.

I've spent my career as a newspaper reporter,

looking smarter thanks to vigilant and talented copyeditors. Katherine Devendorf and Cindy Nixon allowed me to continue that streak with *Barguments*.

I definitely lucked out with Patrick Price, my editor at Simon Spotlight Entertainment. He can spot a good bargument, but I most appreciate his nose for bad ones. You should too—trust me. I knew I was in good shape during our first conversation, when Patrick suggested a bargument category for when you've had too many. *Red or yellow? Up or down?* Stay tuned for the sequel.

Dan Lazar, my agent at Writers House, not only dove onto the *Barguments* bandwagon with gusto, but he took the reins. I've tried to find *Barguments* a publisher since the early 1990s. I think it took Dan three weeks. Even better, he lets me drop cool remarks at bars, like: "My agent retained dramatic rights in Asia, so we'll see how that develops."

Dan also came through with a bargument or two, as did the following friends and family.

Many thanks and a round on me to these bargument pioneers: Allison, Andrew, Becky, Betsy, Billy, Bo, Brad, Brice, Bryna, Caroline, Chad, Cheeks, Chris, Craig, Danet, Danny Mac, Dave, Debbie, Diane, Ditman, Dorward, Ebert, Elizabeth, Emily, Farmar, Glenn, Heather, Holly, Ina, Jane, Javier, Jay (who gets a double for introducing me to Dan), Jed, Jennifer, Jim, Jon, Kate, Katie, K. C., Ken, Kevin, Kristi, Lee, Lewis, Lisa, Liz, Marcia, Mary, Matt, Meredith, Nan, Niala, Nosh, the Other Volmans, Paul, Prosner, Rob, Robin, Roni, Ryan, Sarah, Siachos, Tadd, Todd, Tuck, Valliant, Wes, Wheatley, and Winer.

ABOUT THE AUTHOR

DOUG HANKS lives in Miami and writes for the *Miami Herald.* He has worked as a reporter for several other newspapers, including the *Washington Post*. He still feels certain the lion would win.